All About Planet Earth (Earth Science): First Grade Geography Workbook Series

SPEEDY
PUBLISHING

Speedy Publishing LLC
40 E. Main St. #1156
Newark, DE 19711
www.speedypublishing.com

The Earth is around
4.6 billion years
old according
to scientists.

Earth is the only place in the solar system where life is known to be found.

Earth is often called the ocean planet. Its surface is 70 percent water.

The Earth is
the only planet
that has an
atmosphere
containing
21 percent
oxygen.

Earth doesn't
take 24 hours
to rotate on
its axis. It's
actually
23 hours,
56 minutes and
4 seconds.

Due to Earth's distance from the Sun, it takes about 8 minutes and 19 seconds for light to reach the planet from the Sun.

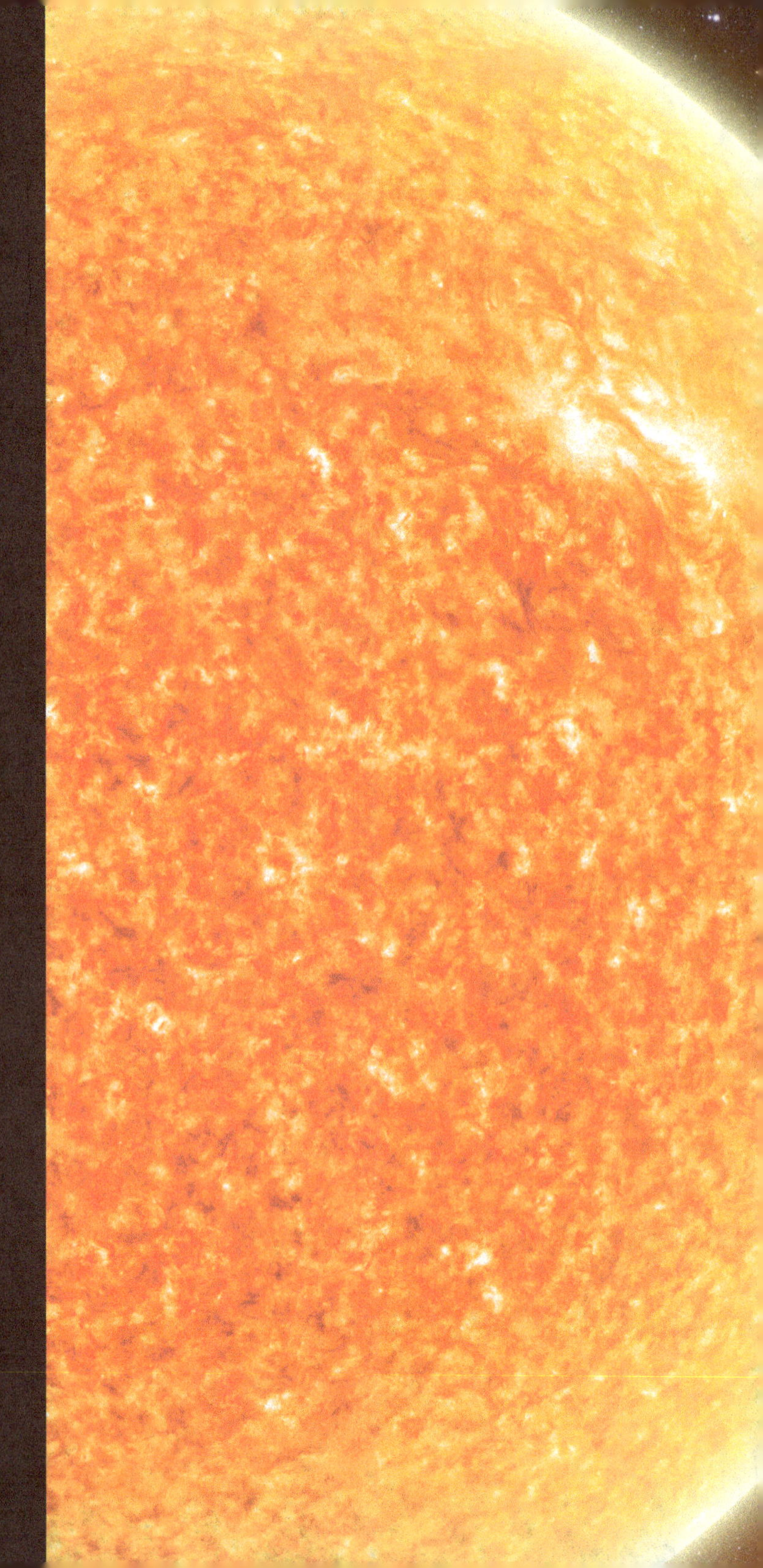

The Earth
orbits the Sun
at a speed of
67,000 miles
per hour.

Earth has 1 moon and 2 additional asteroids locked into a co-orbital orbits with Earth.